PIANO | VOCAL | GUITAR

THE FRAY
SCARS & STORIES

ISBN 978-1-4584-3472-2

HAL•LEONARD®
CORPORATION
7777 W. BLUEMOUND RD. P.O. BOX 13819 MILWAUKEE, WI 53213

In Australia Contact:
Hal Leonard Australia Pty. Ltd.
4 Lentara Court
Cheltenham, Victoria, 3192 Australia
Email: ausadmin@halleonard.com.au

Visit Hal Leonard Online at
www.halleonard.com

CONTENTS

HEARTBEAT

Words and Music by JOSEPH KING
and ISAAC SLADE

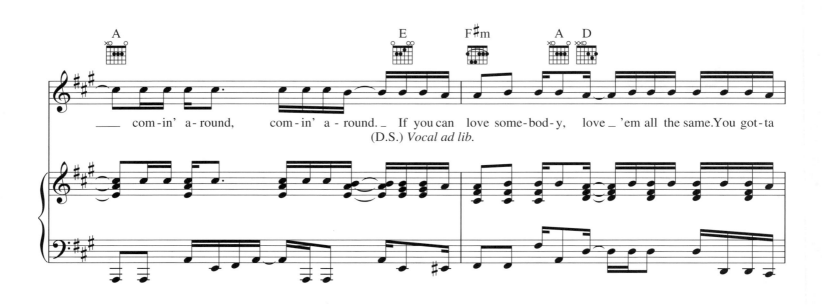

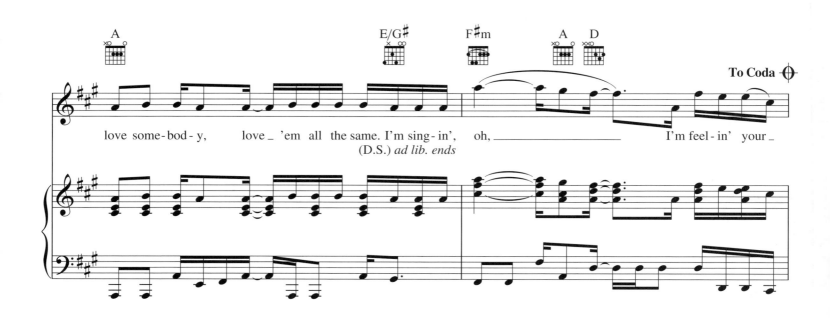

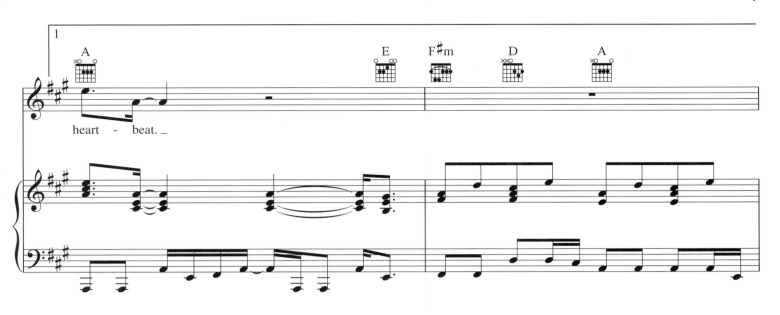

heart - beat. ____

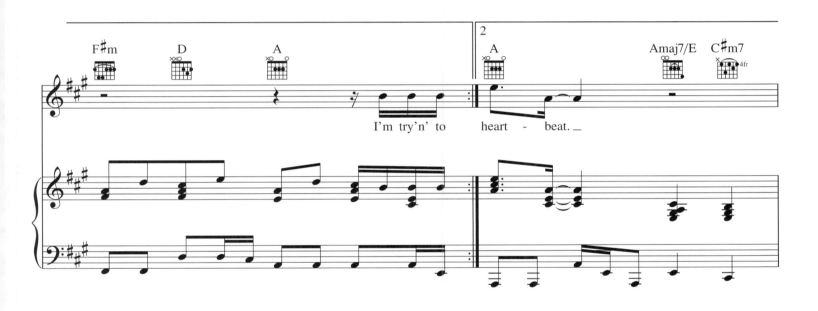

I'm try'n' to heart - beat. ____

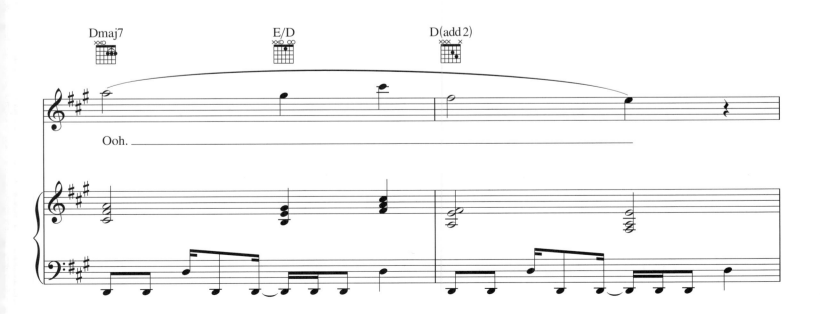

Ooh. ____

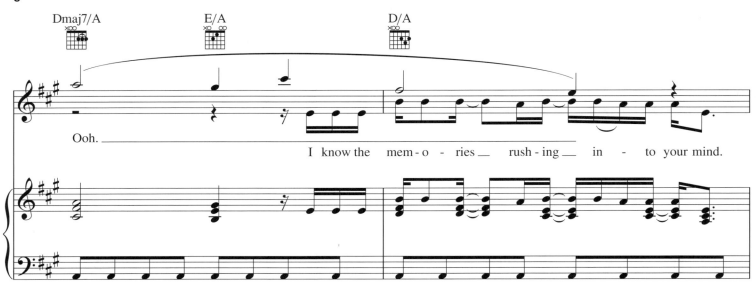

Ooh. _____

I know the mem-o-ries __ rush-ing __ in - to your mind.

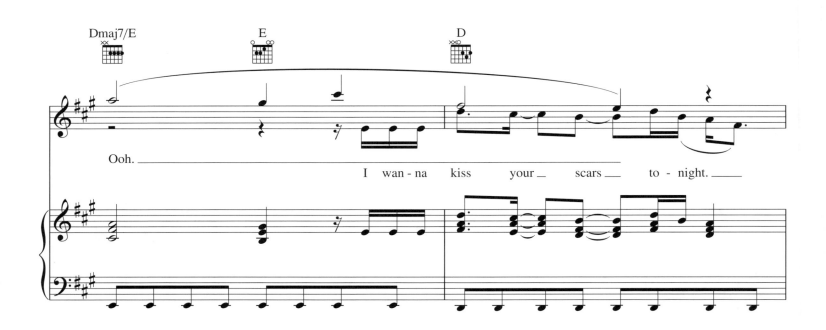

Ooh. _____

I wan-na kiss your __ scars __ to - night. _____

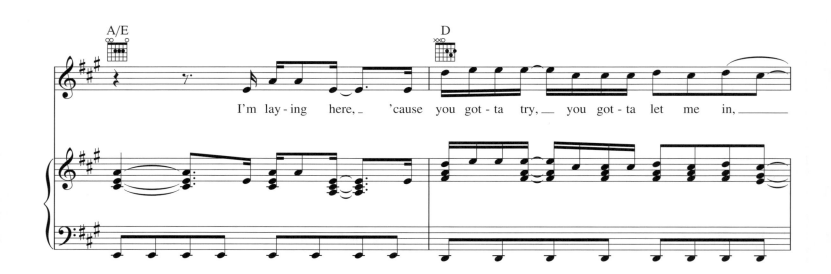

I'm lay-ing here, _ 'cause you got-ta try, __ you got-ta let me in, _____

THE FIGHTER

Words and Music by JOSEPH KING,
ISAAC SLADE, DAVID WELSH
and BEN WYSOCKI

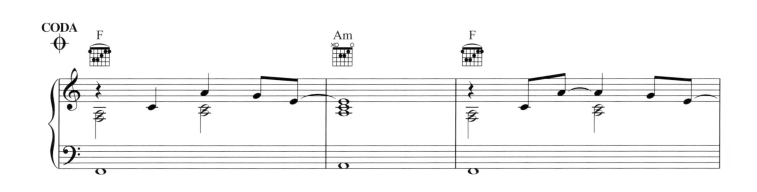

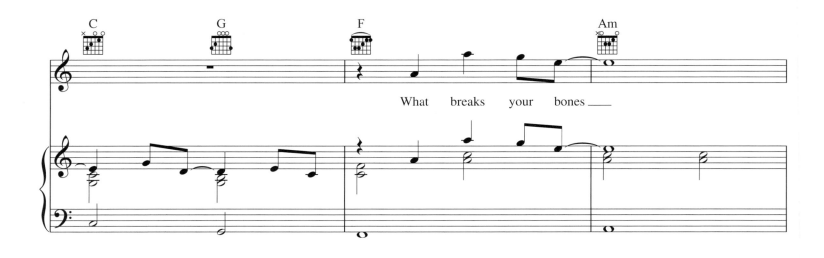

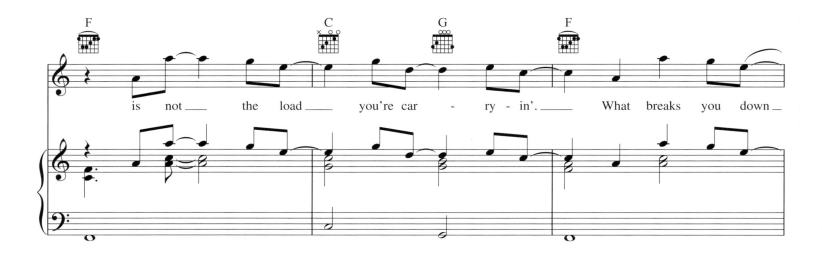

Some - how they both know _____ he's not com - ing home, __ com - ing home. __

TURN ME ON
(Burning)

Words and Music by JOSEPH KING,
ISAAC SLADE, DAVID WELSH
and BEN WYSOCKI

Moderate Funk Rock

There's a sen-tence ___ on my fath-er, ___ on my sis-

-ter ___ and on my broth-er. There's a ter-ror in the cor-

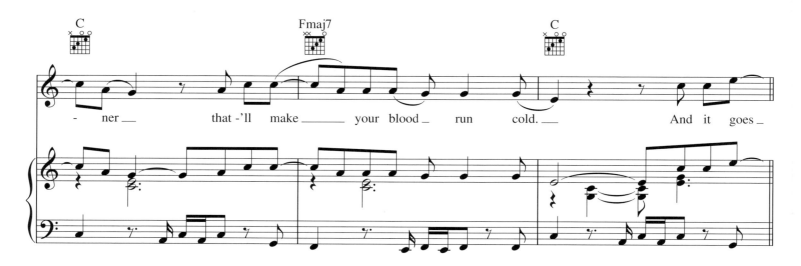

-ner ___ that-'ll make ___ your blood ___ run cold. ___ And it goes ___

RUN FOR YOUR LIFE

Words and Music by JOSEPH KING
and iSAAC SLADE

* Recorded a half step higher.

Run and you don't _____ give up. _____ With
all that you are, _____ all that you want. _____
I will be close _____ be - hind.
Run for your life. _____

THE WIND

Words and Music by JOSEPH KING,
ISAAC SLADE, DAVID WELSH
and BEN WYSOCKI

*Recorded a half step lower.

ooh.

feel the sun ___ com - in' out ___ ris - in' from the ___ east. ___

I

1961

Words and Music by JOSEPH KING
and ISAAC SLADE

I CAN BARELY SAY

Words and Music by JOSEPH KING
and ISAAC SLADE

MUNICH

Words and Music by JOSEPH KING,
ISAAC SLADE, DAVIS WELSH
and BEN WYSOCKI

Take all you know, ___ and you

* *Recorded a half step higher.*

HERE WE ARE

Words and Music by JOSEPH KING,
ISAAC SLADE, DAVID WELSH
and BEN WYSOCKI

N.C.

Instrumental solo

Solo ends

I'm go-in' back and __ forth, __

__ but you're pull - ing __ me in. __ I'm go - ing

48 TO GO

Words and Music by JOSEPH KING,
ISAAC SLADE, DAVID WELSH
and BEN WYSOCKI

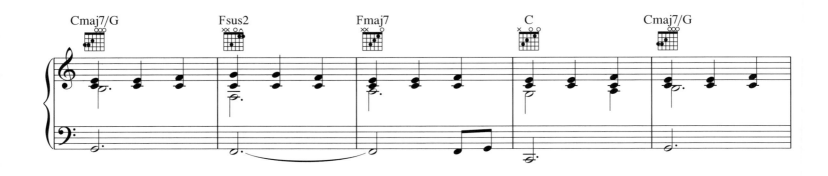

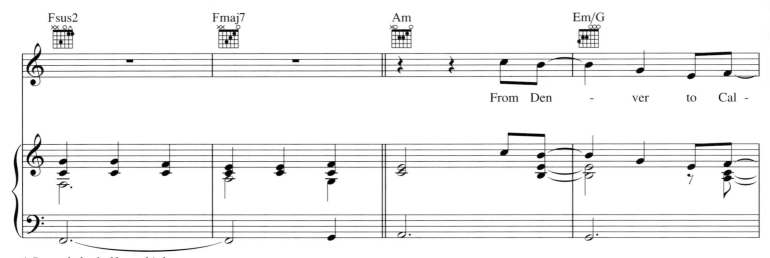

From Den-ver to Cal-

Recorded a half step higher.

RAINY ZURICH

Words and Music by JOSEPH KING
and ISAAC SLADE

In mid-air __ and float-ing off __ to space; __ I'm mov-ing in, __ your hair __
in a down that holds a lone-ly road, __ and the night is fall-ing. There's __

__ is fall-ing all __ a-round __ my ____ face like a par-a-chute. __ I'm
__ a road __ that fol-lows to __ her ____ home, and the sky is heav-y.

Recorded a half step higher.

BE STILL

Words and Music by JOSEPH KING,
ISAAC SLADE, DAVID WELSH
and BEN WYSOCKI